The Digital Nomad Lifestyle

How to Work and Travel the World

Table of Contents

Chapter 1. Introduction

Unshackle yourself from a 9-to-5 office routine, witness the glorious sunsets of Bali, nibble on croissants in a charming Parisian café, or live through a snowy spectacle in the heart of Canada – all while satisfying your professional commitments. Welcome to "The Digital Nomad Lifestyle: How to Work and Travel the World", our exuberant Special Report specially concocted to ignite your wanderlust. Armed with invaluable insights, newbie-friendly tips, and groundbreaking strategies, this is your golden ticket to master the art of working while globetrotting, guiding you to transform an ordinary life into an extraordinary, fulfilling, location-independent journey. Stash away your doubts, bid farewell to convention, and get ready to unravel a life of balance, adventure, and freedom you never thought possible! **Get your copy today and step into the thrilling sphere of digital nomadism.**

Chapter 2. Embracing the Digital Nomad Lifestyle: An Introduction

Welcome, adventurous soul. If you're reading this, chances are you've felt the pull to live a life that's out of the ordinary, to take the path less taken. You've imagined yourself working on a beach, overlooking the ocean as you sip on a smoothie, or coding away at a charming coffee shop in quaint European towns. These dreams not only look vivid in your mind's eye but also sound extremely appealing. The imagery of being a digital nomad tantalizes many, providing a ticket out of the monotonous 9-5 grind. But what exactly is a digital nomad?

2.1. Understanding the Digital Nomad

In essence, a digital nomad is a professional who chooses to work remotely, enabling them to travel and explore different parts of the globe frequently. They're not tied to a fixed location, swapping dull cubicles for a flexible workspace that might include coworking spaces in bustling cities, comfortable coffee shops, beach sides, or serene parks – drawing inspiration from interacting with different cultures, languages, and experiences.

Digital nomads leverage technology advancements and remote working possibilities to its fullest, enabling them to earn a living while enjoying the landscapes and stellar sunsets in Bali or the Nordic landscapes of the Polar Circle. However, it's not just a perpetual vacation. It's about finding a balance between work, recreation, and personal growth while being on the move.

2.2. Breaking Down Some Myths

Before diving in, it's critical to comprehend digital nomadism's realities and discard the myopias popularized by social media. First and foremost, being a digital nomad isn't synonymous with being on a constant holiday. Yes, you might be swapping office cubicles for beachside resorts, but your professional commitments remain.

One of the biggest myths tied to digital nomadism is that it's endlessly glamorous. The filtered Instagram stories and photos seldom highlight the ups and downs of the lifestyle. Time zone differences, occasional feelings of solitude, Wi-Fi connectivity issues, cultural nuances, or language barriers can make work tricky.

Remember, the aim here is not to deter you from nomadism but to present a holistic picture of what this life entails – laying bare both its liberation and challenges.

2.3. The Path to Nomadism

Given the nature of digital nomadism, it's not a path that everyone can tread. It needs a certain level of professional autonomy, flexibility, a sense of adventure, resilience, and above all, a remote-ready job. Many roles across different sectors – from programming, design and education to consultation, writing, and digital marketing – have been adapted to remote work given the rise in digital tools and platorms.

If your current role does not permit remote work, it might be time to upskill, reskill, or pivot to a domain that allows for geographical independence. Leverage online courses, learning platforms, and relevant networks to build a skill set that suits remote work. Remember, it's entirely possible to become a digital nomad within your current line of work, often with some creative strategizing and open discussions with your employer or team.

2.4. Creating a Work-Travel Balance

It's vital to create and maintain a healthy balance between work, travel, and recreation. It could mean grouping tasks in a productive window, scheduling meetings when grounded, or carving out personal time for relaxation or exploring your new surroundings.

Creating structure within the chaos is a key factor every nomad must master. Set defined work hours and follow them religiously. This will not only improve productivity but also give you a clear division between work and personal time, thus allowing you to enjoy your travels without any guilt or worry.

2.5. Nurturing Connections

A significant aspect that often overshadows the appeal of nomadic living is isolation. Sure, you're meeting new people, experiencing new cultures, but the transient nature of your lifestyle might limit the amount of deep, lasting relationships you can foster. Hence, being proactive in staying connected with family, friends, and fellow digital nomads is crucial.

Join online communities, engage in local activities, or attend meetups to create connections and avoid isolation. These interactions not only make your experience feel fuller but also offer you professional insights or collaboration opportunities.

2.6. Learning Through the Lows

Embracing the digital nomad lifestyle involves embracing the highs and the lows. It's essential to learn from challenging situations and build resilience. Technical hiccups, culture shocks, homesickness – these will likely be part of your journey. But they offer invaluable lessons too. With time, you'll hone your adaptability, resilience, and problem-solving skills that'll make this exciting lifestyle sustainable in the long run.

Taking the plunge into digital nomadism is about more than just seeing new places. It is about seriously considering how to incorporate and balance work within your travels. It's about charting a unique life path that aligns with your personal values, desired experiences, and professional aspirations. Is this lifestyle for everyone? Maybe not. But for those who dare to shed the conventional for the extraordinary, who crave for experiences beyond office walls, who find joy in meandering paths, the digital nomad lifestyle could be a fulfilling new chapter, a stepping-stone to a life of freedom, growth, and discovery.

Chapter 3. Turning Nomadic: Preparing for the Transition

Jumping into a nomadic lifestyle can seem like an alluring dream, but there are obstacles that may pose challenges to a soon-to-be nomad. If approached with thorough preparation, transitioning into this lifestyle turns from a mere concept into a practical, achievable reality. So, let's get started with your metamorphosis.

3.1. Understanding the Digital Nomad Lifestyle

Before you make the leap of faith, it's essential to understand what being a digital nomad encompasses. A digital nomad is someone who uses technology to work remotely while traversing the globe. This lifestyle offers ultimate freedom, far from the fixed schedules and physical confines of the traditional workplace. But it comes with its share of challenges, like unstable income, variable living conditions, and potentially unpredictable access to necessities.

Let's debunk two common myths perpetuated about digital nomadism:

1. *Nomadism is a perpetual holiday:* No, you won't spend all day lounging on a beach. It takes discipline and pragmatism to balance work with immersive exploration and cultural experience.

2. *Nomadism is for affluent folks only:* You don't need to hemorrhage money to enjoy this lifestyle. With a well-planned budget and carefully curated locations, the nomadic lifestyle is achievable for most individuals.

3.2. Evaluating Your Current Situation

Before setting sail, appraise your present circumstances. Are you satisfied with your job? Are there ties that could hinder your transition? Be brutally honest with yourself. Make a list of factors you need to consider, like current job satisfaction, financial stability, family obligations, and personal relationships. Weight them appropriately. These will serve as your guides for the transition.

3.3. Deciding Your Source of Income

Arguably the most crucial consideration is your means of livelihood. Several avenues can generate income while traveling–the most common being remote jobs, freelancing, and entrepreneurship. You might already have a remote-friendly job that allows you to morph into a digital nomad with minimal fuss. If not, it's time to explore other possibilities. Freelancing services like writing, designing, marketing, and teaching can provide a flexible income stream. Alternatively, entrepreneur opportunities like eCommerce, dropshipping, or franchising might interest you. Keep in mind, transitioning to a new income source often requires time and effort, so plan accordingly.

3.4. Setting a Realistic Budget

Now that you've decided on an income source, it's time to have a clear, accurate budget in place. Consider costs like travel expenses, accommodation, meals, health care, and recreational activities when setting up your budget. Make sure to include an emergency fund to handle unexpected situations. Aim for a frugal yet comfortable lifestyle where you can explore your surroundings without pinching pennies at every step.

3.5. Preparing to Let Go

As you start preparing for the transition, you will need to let go of some things. Begin decluttering your possessions. Understand that your whole home cannot come with you. Sell, donate, or store away items that you will not need on the journey. Accept that you will trade in a portion of your physical stability for more freedom and adventure.

3.6. Adaptability and Open-Mindedness

Embrace adaptability. Soon, you'll be in places where they don't speak your language, where the food is alien, and customs are different. An open mind will help you embrace new cultures and experiences. Remember, this lifestyle is as much about self-improvement and personal growth as it is about exploring new countries and cultures.

3.7. Cultivating your Digital Skills

Although being a digital nomad does not require you to be a tech geek, understanding some fundamental digital tools can take you a long way. Be familiar with productivity applications, communication tools, project management software, and the basics of digital security. These are vital skills if your work involves client interaction and collaboration.

3.8. Maintaining a Healthy Lifestyle

Lastly, but most importantly, bear in mind that your health remains a priority. Establish a routine that incorporates exercise and a balanced diet. Whether it's yoga on a seaside resort, a run through a city park, or simple indoor workouts, figure out what works for you. Understanding local cuisines and their nutritional value is also beneficial.

Embarking on a journey of digital nomadism is exhilarating. The preparations and decisions might seem intimidating at first, but once you're on the road, living your dreams, you'll know the time and effort invested in proper planning was worth it. The transition to digital nomadism is an incredible journey of self-exploration and world exploration. Embrace these preparations as the initial steps of this unforgettable adventure!

Chapter 4. Choosing Your Portable Profession: In-Demand Jobs for Digital Nomads

The wonderful, intriguing thing about our modern digital age is the endless opportunities it presents to work from any corner of the globe. The digital nomad lifestyle becomes even more feasible with a profession that effortlessly aligns with this futuristic ideal. Herein lies the importance of selecting a portable profession, ensuring your work goes with you where you journey.

4.1. Identifying the Right Job For You

Begin by understanding your skills, interests, and training. A self-assessment will clarify what roles you're best suited for.

It's not mandatory to be a seasoned professional or a longtime freelancer to embark on this journey. The critical element is your desire to acquire new skills, your willingness to embrace change and an undying approach to learning.

4.2. Learning a Digital Nomad Friendly Skill

It's imperative to be familiar and adept with digital skills. Digital literacy opens up a spectrum of opportunities that might not have been perceived as possible a decade ago. An investment in acquiring or refining digital skills such as coding, marketing, designing, writing or teaching can transform your work life, enabling you to perform your professional duties from anywhere in the world.

4.3. Programming and Coding

The world of programming and coding offers diverse opportunities. From web development and software programming to data analysis, the field is vast. Being able to develop and maintain websites or create software programs places you in a position where location is irrelevant.

One of the key benefits as a programmer is your ability to work on numerous freelance platforms and your adaptability in collaborative technologies such as Github or Bitbucket. Apart from freelancing, remote job opportunities abound in companies looking to trim office costs while acquiring tech talent globally.

4.4. Digital Marketing

The scope of digital marketing is unimaginably large. A number of sub-fields within this discipline offer outstanding remote work opportunities. Experts in search engine optimization (SEO), social media management, content creation, email marketing, pay-per-click (PPC) advertising and other digital marketing niches are in high demand.

The beauty of digital marketing is that it does not confine you to a specific industry. The principles can be transferred and incorporated across various industries allowing you great diversity in your work.

4.5. Graphic Designing and Multimedia Production

If you're inclined towards the creative side, graphic designing is another field ripe with opportunities. From brand identity creation to designing marketing collateral, the demand for well-designed visual communication is high.

Joining the creative brigade is multimedia production. If creating engaging video content or recording podcasts is your forte, you're in luck. With platforms like YouTube and Spotify booming, there's increased demand for video editors, sound technicians and other multimedia professionals.

4.6. Writing and Editing

If expressing thoughts through words is your strength, writing and editing could be your foolproof method to nomadic living. From blog management and copywriting to transcription and proofreading, there are various niches to explore.

Content is king in the online world. As long as businesses require content to captivate audiences, the demand for skilled writers and editors will remain consistently high.

4.7. Virtual Teaching and Tutoring

The e-learning industry has skyrocketed. Virtual tutoring and online teaching, in subjects like languages, sciences, or music to name a few, are gaining substantial traction.

Through platforms like Coursera, Udemy, or even personalized one-on-one classes online, you can connect with students around the world. What better way to utilize your knowledge and passion for teaching than by sharing them with keen learners globally?

4.8. Consulting

If you are an expert in a particular skill or industry, consulting can ensure a dependable living. As a consultant, you advise clients on streamlining their operations, making informed decisions, reducing costs, and enhancing revenue prospects. With virtual communication tools, consulting knows no boundaries.

4.9. Identifying Remote Jobs

Finding jobs that offer remote work is critical for pursuing the digital nomad lifestyle. Websites like Remote.co, FlexJobs, and WeWorkRemotely are excellent resources to find work. Many companies are embracing the remote work phenomenon, making the possibility of a digital nomad experience more achievable than ever.

Remember, the best portable professions align with your skills and aspirations. Try out a variety of vocations until you settle on a profession that you can perform remotely with full passion and commitment. The luxury of balancing work and play, and relishing the fruits of digital nomadism will follow naturally.

Chapter 5. Staying Connected: Essential Tech and Tools for Work On-the-go

Internet connectivity and regular access to the right pieces of technology are the lifeblood of successful digital nomadism. Constant movement means you need the right tools to stay grounded, and staying professionally active requires a balance of portability and power when it comes to your tech lineup.

5.1. Electronic Gadgets

First and foremost, let's start with electronic gadgets. The pairing of a powerful laptop and a smart mobile device is foundational for any digital nomad. Your choices will largely depend on your specific needs, so let's cover the essential categories of electronic gadgets you should consider.

1. Laptop: A portable, powerful laptop that is equipped with all necessary software for your work is essential. It can be a PC or Mac, depending on your preference. Ensure that the battery life is long-lasting, as you may often be working in locations that do not provide instant power supply.

2. Smartphone: A robust, high-speed smartphone can serve as a backup device for work when you can't use your laptop. In addition, it also allows you to navigate, translate, and access handy local information when exploring new places.

3. External Drive: For backup and additional storage, an external hard drive is indispensable. Losing data when you are halfway across the world can be catastrophic. To mitigate this risk, consider backing up your most crucial files to an external hard drive.

4. Portable Charger/Power Bank: A portable charger is vital, especially when power outlets are scarce or when there's no time to fully charge your devices. Consider your power requirements for all gadgets before purchasing.

5. Adaptors and Converters: Most countries have unique plug shapes and voltage. Verify the type your destination uses and pack the appropriate adaptors and converters to maintain your gadgets' operation.

5.2. Connectivity Solutions

Without robust internet access, even the most powerful laptop or the smartest phone may seem useless. Consider these options to ensure a persistent and reliable internet connection.

1. International Data Plan: Most phone carriers offer international data plans. If you travel frequently, it's worth investing in an international data plan so you can have access to the internet almost wherever you go.

2. Local SIM Cards: These are often an affordable way to access the internet. Pay-as-you-go SIM cards can provide flexibility, especially if you'll be in a single location for a few weeks or months.

3. Portable WiFi Device: This portable gadget allows you to access the internet in over 100 countries. It's a great option to maintain connectivity, especially in locations where mobile data is unreliable.

4. Co-working Spaces: They often offer facilities such as desks, meeting rooms, and importantly, fast and reliable internet. Even in remote locations, you may find co-working spaces geared towards digital nomads.

5.3. Useful Applications and Software

Transitioning smoothly to a digital nomad lifestyle is partly facilitated by exploiting the best technology has to offer.

1. Virtual Private Network (VPN): A VPN boosts your online security and allows access to geo-restricted content. Safety must be a priority when dealing with sensitive, work-related content online.

2. Organization and Productivity Tools: Trello, Asana, Google Suite, MS Teams, and Slack are popular for managing tasks, sharing files, and communicating with teams. These apps also have phone counterparts for working on-the-go.

3. Travel Apps: Local apps for navigation, translation, rideshare, food delivery can save you time and effort. Examples include Google Maps, Uber, and Duolingo.

4. Cloud Backup: Google Drive, Dropbox, and OneDrive are examples of cloud storage providers where you can store, sync, and share your files across various devices and users.

5.4. Device Security Measures

Finally, ensuring your device's security is imperative as it guarantees both the safety of your work and personal data.

1. Regular Backups: Regularly backing up your data ensures its availability even if your device is stolen or suffers from a system failure.

2. Theft Protection: Install theft-protection software like Prey or Undercover, which can help trace your device if it's stolen.

3. Two-Factor Authentication: Enable this on all your accounts. It

adds an extra layer of security by requiring two types of identification.

4. Antivirus: Install a robust antivirus solution to protect your devices from malware.

Remember, the goal is to empower your work-life with the right technology while traveling, ensuring convenience and effectiveness. Understanding your unique requirements and carefully selecting from the wide array of available tools can maximize your output, security, and overall digital nomad experience. Explore, test, and optimize your tech lineup as your adventure in digital nomadism unfolds!

Chapter 6. Mastering Time Management: Balancing Work and Exploration

Time is an elusive commodity, especially when your work and living environment is a labyrinth of foreign cultures, cuisines, architectures, and landscapes waiting to be explored. It's easy to get lost in the immersive nature of travel. Yet, as a digital nomad, it's quintessential to strike a balance between your professional commitments and urge to discover the world.

6.1. Understanding Time

Before you embark on your digital nomad journey, it's imperative to understand the essential qualities of time itself. Time is continuous, it can't be stored for later use, and every second wasted is a second gone forever. Digital nomads often face the challenge of managing time across different time zones, especially when collaborating with global teams. Hence, understanding the essence of managing time is the initial step towards balancing work and exploration.

6.2. Time Zones and Scheduling

One major stumbling block a digital nomad faces is traversing multiple time zones. It is quite likely that while you're lapping up the sun on an exotic beach, your clients or colleagues might be burning the midnight oil. Use world time converter tools to work around this issue and align your work schedule effectively.

Taking the time zone of your home base or clients into consideration, schedule important work-related activities, video calls, or deadlines. Always remember – during collaborations, it's not just about your convenience. It's best to be flexible and adjust your work hours whenever necessary to cater to your partners.

6.3. Setting Priorities: Work First or Travel First?

For some, working in the early mornings might be preferable, allowing them to spend the rest of the day exploring. Others might prefer getting lost in a new city during the day and immersing themselves in work during the quieter evenings. Neither approaches are wrong. But it's essential to prioritize and tailor the routine based on your individual productivity cycles.

6.4. The Power of Routine

Establishing a routine is crucial. Structuring your day will help you make the most out of your work hours, leaving more time to explore and experience the location. Start by determining your most productive hours, then allot them to work-related activities. Fill the remaining hours with relaxation and exploration.

6.5. Tools that Aid Time Management

Various apps and tools can assist you in managing time effectively. Time-tracking tools like Toggl or Harvest can help you understand how you spend your working hours, providing insight into your productivity patterns. Scheduling tools such as Google Calendar or Asana can help manage deadlines and appointments.

6.6. The Art of Saying 'No'

As enchanting as novelty experiences or networking events might seem, sometimes it's essential to say 'no'. Prioritize your to-do list and make sure work commitments aren't overlooked amidst the allure of new ventures.

6.7. The Weekend Mindset: Beating the Weekend Rush

Tourist spots are notoriously busy during weekends. One advantage of a digital nomad lifestyle is unconventional workweek patterns. Arrange to explore popular spots during weekdays, when they are likely quieter, leaving less populated or relaxing activities for the weekend. This arrangement not only maximizes your exploratory experience but also allows for a more flexible work schedule.

6.8. Preserving 'Me Time'

Maintaining personal time for self-care is essential. This includes exercise, meditation, reading, or anything that helps you unwind and relax. Remember, the aim is not just balancing work and exploration, but also maintaining personal well-being to ensure a sustainable digital nomad lifestyle.

6.9. The Power of Adaptability

A significant component of time management is adaptability. As digital nomads, unexpected changes are the rule rather than the exception. Skills such as quick decision-making and responsive rearrangements can make the difference in proficient time management.

Achieving a perfect balance between work and exploration as a digital nomad might not happen overnight. Persistence, adaptability, and incorporating an effective time-management strategy will aid in adjusting to this lifestyle. Remember, the goal isn't to whip up a rigid timetable, binding you to a tiresome monotonous regime. Instead, the aim is to provide a flexible framework which, while ensuring your professional commitments are met, also allows for maximum exploration and personal growth. Embrace this approach, and you'll find managing time as a digital nomad both fulfilling and rewarding.

Chapter 7. Navigating Global Finances: Money Management while Abroad

Moving across the globe, exploring different cultures, and immersing yourself in the colors of the world – the life of a digital nomad seems like a dream come true. However, it's not all sunshine and rainbows. There's one crucial aspect that, while often overlooked amidst the thrill of adventure, forms the very backbone of this lifestyle: financial management. And for the globe-trotters among us, this paints a more convoluted picture. So, let's dive into the intricacies of managing your global finances as a digital nomad.

7.1. Understanding Currency Exchange Rates

One of the most critical financial aspects a digital nomad will encounter is currency exchange. Before stepping foot in your next destination, you must ascertain the exchange rate of your home currency versus the local one. This knowledge will be useful in preventing overspending and understanding your purchasing power in the new location.

Now, you'd find numerous online platforms and apps offering real-time exchange rates. A few reliable sources include XE, OANDA, and Forex. Additionally, it's wise to keep updated with global financial news. Factors like national incidents, political decisions, and shifts in the economy can greatly impact exchange rates.

7.2. Handling Cash and Card Transactions

While it may be an existing habit to utilize credit or debit cards, this may not always be feasible. Some regions favor cash transactions over plastic, and in others, the transaction or withdrawal fees for foreign cards can be high. It's critical to research beforehand.

A wise strategy is to carry a reasonable amount of cash for immediate expenses upon arriving in a new country. Always carry more than one card from different international banking networks, such as Visa, Mastercard, or American Express. This act ensures you have a backup should one card fail or not be accepted.

Beware of Dynamic Currency Conversion (DCC). While abroad, merchants or ATMs might offer to charge transactions in your home currency rather than the local one. Decline this offer because the conversion rates of DCC are typically inflated.

7.3. Choosing the Right Bank

Choosing an international-friendly bank can save you a lot of money in withdrawal fees and unfavorable exchange rates. Online banks like Revolut, N26, or Charles Schwab are popular among digital nomads for their nominal fees and useful functionalities.

Look for banks that offer no foreign transaction fees, low or no ATM withdrawal fees, robust online banking features, and excellent customer support. As for selecting the right credit card, prioritize cards that come with air miles, insurance coverage, and other beneficial rewards for travellers.

7.4. Fintech and Mobile Banking Apps

The rise of fintech has blessed digital nomads with an array of mobile banking apps easing the burden of managing finances globally. Research, choose, and use an app that best fits your needs.

Whether it be TransferWise for low-cost international money transfers, Mint for budgeting and tracking expenses, or Robinhood for dabbling in investments, these apps prove to be essential tools in a digital nomad's arsenal.

7.5. Decoding Taxes

Possibly the most complex and dreaded part of managing finances abroad is understanding and keeping up with tax obligations. Being a digital nomad doesn't exempt you from paying taxes. The details, however, are dependent on your nationality, residency status, income, and where you earn your income.

Seek professional help to comprehend tax laws. Consider hiring international tax consulting services or using platforms like Taxes for Expats. Do note, failing to comply with your tax responsibilities can result in serious penalties or legal trouble.

7.6. Creating a Sustainable Budget

A sustainable budget is the cornerstone to manage your finances effectively. Include all possible expenses, such as accommodation, food, travel, health insurance, taxes, and ensure to add a buffer for unexpected expenditures. Tools like Trail Wallet, Toshl Finance, or You Need a Budget (YNAB) can make budgeting feel like less of a chore.

Remember, being financially self-reliant and responsibly managing your finances isn't merely beneficial but essential for life as a digital nomad. Create the wandering life of your dreams but be sure to stay financially grounded whilst you do so. It's a fine, yet achievable, balance.

Chapter 8. Mental Health on the Road: Mitigating Loneliness and Burnout

Chapter 9. Staying Connected

The digital nomad lifestyle undeniably offers an unbeatable feeling of freedom and independence. Yet, it is essential to acknowledge that humans innately crave social connections. This need doesn't necessarily vanish once you trade your traditional office space for the untamed vistas of the world. No matter how enriching your travel experiences might be, there could be moments where the absence of familiar faces might feel overwhelming. This section will explore various ways to maintain social interactions and stay connected, mitigating the feelings of loneliness that may creep in during your globetrotting journey.

9.1. Embrace Local Cultures

Engaging with local cultures and communities provides an excellent opportunity to connect with others and root yourself in the social fabric of new locations. It could mean participating in traditional festivals, attending local meetups, or simply striking up conversations with locals at a café.

9.2. Digital Communities and Co-Working Spaces

Digitization not only supports remote work but also digital communities. Numerous platforms connect digital nomads worldwide, providing a virtual space for sharing experiences, resources, and companionship. Joining these communities can offer a sense of belonging that tempers feelings of isolation. Similarly, co-working spaces offer physical communal environments where you can mingle with like-minded individuals while working.

Chapter 10. Managing Stress and Preventing Burnout

As exciting as a digital nomad lifestyle might seem, it can also be volatile, leading to stress and potential burnout if not properly managed. It's crucial to develop a strategy to manage this stress and maintain mental balance.

10.1. Maintaining a Regular Routine

It might seem counterintuitive, but for a life of constant travel, cultivating a routine can provide a sense of normalcy and structure, mitigating stress. This routine can include exercise, regular work hours, and consistent meal times. Despite switching locations, if some elements of your daily life remain consistent, it's easier to build stability and maintain mental health.

10.2. Physical Health and Exercise

Physical health significantly impacts mental well-being. As a digital nomad, opportunities for exercise might vary depending on your location – but there are always possibilities. This could mean hiking in the mountains of Nepal, surfing in Australia, or practicing yoga in Thailand. Regular physical activity is a proven stress reliever, and it helps to keep any anxious thoughts at bay.

10.3. Mindfulness and Meditation

Practicing mindfulness helps manage stress, allowing you to stay grounded amidst the unpredictability of the nomad lifestyle. By directing your attention to the present, you can distance yourself from undue worries about the future and regrets about the past.

There are numerous mindfulness practices you could adopt, like meditation, breathing exercises, or simply spending quiet time in nature.

Chapter 11. Establishing Work-Life Balance

When your work and personal life share the same space, it's easy to blur boundaries. Establishing a proper balance is crucial for keeping burnout at bay. You must remind yourself that you are more than your profession and dedicate time for relaxation and exploration based on this understanding.

11.1. Setting Clear Boundaries

Setting boundaries involves creating explicit demarcations between your work time and personal time. It's easy to fall into the trap of working round the clock when your office is just a laptop away. Make conscious decisions to clock out at a particular time and resist checking work-related communication during off hours.

11.2. Time Management and Prioritization

Learning to manage your time well is integral to establishing a work-life balance. Efficient time management allows you to complete your professional tasks within allocated periods, leaving you with sufficient leisure time. Prioritization is key – focus on tasks that matter the most and are time-sensitive. Investing in digital tools and apps could be a practical way to assist your time management efforts and help avoid work-time intrusions into personal time.

Chapter 12. Seeking Professional Help

Despite our best efforts, there may be times when feelings of loneliness, stress or burnout become overwhelming. At such moments, seeking help from a mental health professional can provide the necessary support and guidance to navigate through these challenges.

12.1. Teletherapy and Online Counseling

Thanks to advancement in technology, professional mental health support is now available online. Teletherapy and online counseling are effective ways to reach out to therapists, counselors, or psychologists, especially when you are travelling between different locations. It can provide essential emotional support when you need it, irrespective of where you are in the world.

In conclusion, it's crucial to remember that a digital nomad lifestyle does not inherently lead to loneliness and burnout. However, the unique set of challenges it poses requires you to be proactive about your mental health. Applying these strategies can help ensure a positive, fulfilling digital nomad experience.

Chapter 13. Legal Aspects and Visas: Overcoming Bureaucratic Hurdles

Venturing into the world of digital nomadism can be a thrilling concept. To transmute this exciting idea into reality requires understanding less adventurous facets of this free-flowing lifestyle as well, most significantly, the rigmarole of legalities and visa requirements. With preparation, patience, and a hint of finesse, these seeming obstacles can be transformed into detailed roadmaps guiding your gallivanting journey.

13.1. Understanding the Legal Framework

Before jetting off to your dream destination, it's imperative to understand the legal framework of remote work. There's a thin line between traveling and living abroad, and it's crucial not to transgress these legal boundaries. Here's a detailed review of the essential legal aspects to consider:

1. Data Security: Employers fundamentally value the security and confidentiality of their data. Ensure that your workload doesn't involve sharing sensitive details via insecure platforms. Consider using VPNs, secure email clients, and cloud storage with high encryption standards for optimal data protection.

2. Taxation: Navigating the maze of global taxation is no mean feat. Aim to understand your tax obligations both in your home country and abroad. Some nations have tax treaties to prevent dual taxation. Consulting with a tax attorney or a freelance tax expert could prove highly beneficial.

3. Contracts and Agreements: Have the scope of your work and legal obligations clearly defined and agreed upon in a contract. This elucidates expectations from both parties, responsibilities, and payment terms, safeguarding you against potential misunderstandings and disputes.

13.2. Navigating Through Visa Regulations

Visa regulations differ from country to country, and understanding them is a prerequisite for your digital nomad journey. Here, we delve into the various types of visas and their implications:

1. Tourist Visa: Most countries require foreign nationals to enter their borders with a valid tourist visa. Although these visas do not permit paid work, many digital nomads work on such permits presuming remote work doesn't contravene the rule. However, this is deemed a legal gray area and can lead to complications. It's essential to thoroughly read the terms of the tourist visa and seek legal advice if unsure.

2. Business Visa: Business visas are often secured by digital nomads for temporary work. These visas cover you to attend meetings, seminars, and occasionally, short term contracts. Their duration varies from a few weeks to a year.

3. Work Visa: Work visas are a safer and more lawful route. Securing a work visa generally means demonstrating that your employment will contribute to the local economy, which might be challenging for some digital nomads. However, some countries embrace this lifestyle and have created special work visas, known as "Digital Nomad Visas", for independent foreign remote workers.

13.3. A Deep-dive into Digital Nomad Visas

Recently, several nations have recognized the shifts in global work cultures and introduced Digital Nomad Visas. These allow foreign nationals to reside in the country and legally work for a company abroad.

1. Estonia: Estonia offers a Digital Nomad Visa that allows remote workers and their families to live in Estonia for up to a year. Applicants must prove that they can work location-independently and meet the minimum income threshold.

2. Barbados: On The Barbados Welcome Stamp, digital nomads can live and work for up to one year. To qualify, you must show evidence of work with an overseas company or your own company registered abroad.

3. Bali, Indonesia: Bali has announced plans to introduce a Digital Nomad visa, allowing foreign residents to live and work on the famous 'Island of Gods' legally.

13.4. Overcoming Bureaucratic Hurdles

To expedite bureaucratic processes, consider the following tactics:

1. Documentation: Be diligent to provide all the necessary paperwork accurately and in time. This includes filled application forms, passport-sized photographs, valid passports, proofs of accommodations, return tickets, and financial solvency.

2. Research: Always stay updated about recent changes in visa policies and thoroughly understand the application process.

3. Consultation: Engage a legal consultant or visa expert to assist

you through the visa application procedures. Their expertise can help avoid potential pitfalls, and their familiarity with the process can smooth out the application journey.

Navigating the crossroads of legalities and worldwide travel can be daunting, but remember, behind every successful digital nomad lies a well-organized, thorough plan. Understanding and abiding by the legal aspects of your globetrotter life facilitate a breezy, worry-free voyage as you venture towards your next exciting remote work hub!

Chapter 14. Building a Global Network: Community and Connections in Nomadic Life

Every fervent anticipation of exploring foreign lands and immersing in unfamiliar cultures accompanies an often-underestimated requirement: building a global network to thrive in the digital nomad lifestyle. Your journey towards becoming a self-sufficient marvel, curating work, travel, and personal growth simultaneously, pivots significantly on the community and connections you form.

14.1. Why Build a Global Network?

Lone ventures into uncharted territories can be gratifying, but the power of fruitful connections and a supportive community shouldn't be undervalued. Embracing connections, both from your hometown and from abroad, can deliver an unmatched amalgamation of perspectives, ideas, support, and camaraderie. Networking with like-minded individuals or clusters provides not only friendships but also professional collaborations, customer bases, mentors, and sources of inspiration.

Navigating a new city's do's and don'ts, its hidden gems, or forging partnerships with local businesses become untangled with insider insights. Furthermore, building a global network accelerates your assimilation into foreign societies, helping you steer clear of isolation and foster local engagement while reinforcing your professional standing internationally.

14.2. Understanding the Power of Meaningful Connections

In the competitive landscape of freelancing or digital businesses, having a robust international network provides a strategic edge to secure clientele, collaborations, or job opportunities that go beyond geographic boundaries. An expansive network broadens visibility and learning opportunities, catalyzing professional growth.

Personal connections also hold profound value, contributing significantly to enriching experiences. They offer emotional support, lighten the burden of loneliness, help in overcoming various hurdles, and can transform your journey into a collective, multifaceted voyage of growth and joy. It's the shared meal in a traditional Malaysian household, the impromptu Salsa lesson in Santiago, or the language exchange with an Italian amico. These connections color your digital nomad lifestyle, morphing it from a singular, work-conducive, travel-hungry pursuit to a globally-connected, culturally immersive experience.

14.3. Networking in a Digital Age

Digital tools have made communicating with netizens across the globe as easy as the click of a button. Online platforms present limitless scopes for connection-building and are instrumental in fostering your nomadic network. Social networking websites like Facebook, LinkedIn or curated spaces, such as various digital nomad forums, Slack workspaces, or WhatsApp groups, are teeming with potential connections (clients, fellow nomads, mentors) ready to be tapped.

Engaging in online communities specific to your industry or interests can offer crucial pointers, job leads, or be a space for sharing challenges and solutions. Don't shy away from cold outreach on

LinkedIn or Twitter. A polite, personal message expressing mutual interest can launch a beneficial exchange of ideas or partnerships. Be proactive and a courteous digital citizen, and your network will surely grow.

14.4. Embrace Local and In-Person Networking

While the digital sphere immensely aids global networking, in-person networking forms the heart of truly enriching connections. Be present, attend local events or festivals, join workshops, or language exchange meetings. Participate in co-working spaces or frequent local haunts, be it the charming corner café or the community yoga class.

Depending on your location, there are various networks for digital nomads to join. These include Meetup groups, InterNations, or city-specific digital nomad communities. Explore these options and take an active participant role for maximal benefit.

14.5. Organize & Attend Events

Unleash a proactive spirit and organize or attend events, meetups, or conferences relevant to your industry or personal interests. Participating in industry-specific conferences can be rewarding, attributing opportunities for knowledge sharing, collaboration, client-scouting, and potential job leads.

Smaller scale meetups, informal gatherings, or themed events offer spaces for authentic one-on-one connections and shared experiences. Consider platforms like Meetup.com or Eventbrite to discover events in your vicinity or to curate your own.

14.6. Establishing Authentic Connections

Building a global network isn't a mere numbers game; it's about establishing genuine connections, where mutual growth and support lie at the cornerstone. Focus on showing authentic interest, offer help before you seek, and engage in meaningful conversations. Befriend locals, fellow nomads, entrepreneurs, expats—every individual holds a novel perspective and unique knack that can inspire both personal and professional growth.

14.7. Achieving a Balance

Flourishing in the digital nomad lifestyle is about balancing glorious sunset-chasing with nurturing hearty connections. Equal emphasis on work, exploration, and networking ensures a robust global network, transforming your journey into a fulfilling, community-anchored narrative.

Explore thoughtfully, network generously, and live vividly as you venture into the incredible realms of digital nomadism. The world indeed becomes your oyster, enthused with rich connections, global friendships, inspiring collaborations while you steer your professional voyage across the world map. Balance is your key to unlock the harmonizing melody of a digital nomad's life, beautifully intertwined with work, travel, and networking.

Global networking isn't an overnight feat but a rewarding journey reaped with patience, authenticity, and a dash of adventurism. May your digital nomad path be colored with diverse encounters, supportive communities, enriching exchanges, and successful collaborations, strengthening your global presence while you traverse palatial mountains, vast oceans, and hustle in your global office.

When going global, remember that everywhere is connected. From Bali's serene rice paddies to the bustling market squares of Marrakech, from the skyscraping towers of New York to the tranquil Tatras of Slovakia, every corner of the world brings you an opportunity for connection, offering a unique resonance to enrich your digital nomad symphony. Forge meaningful bonds, aimed not just at checking off a must-visit list, but also at weaving a global narrative of shared communities, connections, and collective growth. Step firmly into the world of digital nomadism, nurtured not in isolation but thriving amidst a global, connected network. Remember, your nomadic journey is as rich and fulfilling as your global connections are.

To conclude, there is strength found in numbers, but there is immense power found in connections. As a digital nomad, making links across continents goes beyond professional networking. It is about creating a reliable, diverse support system. The rich tapestry of these connections weave an enriching narrative to your digital nomad life, enabling you to live out a balanced, adventure-filled, and fulfilling journey. When embarking on your digital nomad expedition, always keep this in mind – the world is your office, and its people, your comrades. Let your journey be empowered by this global network, and let it, in turn, fortify your life with new opportunities, experiences, and life-long friendships. Remember, we are, after all, citizens of the world.

Chapter 15. Living the Dream: Real-Life Stories of Successful Digital Nomads

To truly envisage the allure of the digital nomad lifestyle, there is no better way than diving into real-life narratives - footprints left by those who braved this unconventional path. Let's explore what their new-age entrepreneurship entailed, the highs, the lows, and everything in between.

15.1. From Hedge Funds to Jungle Huts: The Tale of Simon

Simon, a former hedge fund manager from London, swapped his office cubicle and busy-crowded-city setting for the sandy beaches of Bali. Leaving behind a plush six-figure salary, Simon turned his passion for wildlife photography into a profession. He initially started blogging, gaining income through ads and sponsorships. He then expanded into selling prints and providing workshops, exploring the rich flora and fauna of the Asian islands. Simon admits to the difficulties he faced initially, particularly with the reduced income. However, the intangible dividends—freedom, adventure, connections—made his journey worthwhile. Today, he lives in an eco-friendly jungle hut, contributing to conserving his new home while earning a living - a beautiful synergy of work, passion, and lifestyle.

15.2. Designing Life's Palette: Sara's Story

Next on the journey of real-life narratives is Sara, a graphic designer from New York who transformed the world into her canvas. After winning a design competition with a cryptocurrency startup, the company offered her a full-time remote role. She happily accepted it, packed her life into a backpack, and embarked on her journey. Originally focused on Europe, she found coworking spaces a blessing, allowing her to meet like-minded individuals and prospective clients. Her portfolio expanded organically over time, now transcending various industries and continents. She admits that Wi-Fi-dependency once left her stranded ahead of a deadline, but such risks, she believes, are offset by the richness of experiences she gains.

15.3. Off the Beaten Path: Adrian, The Non-Tech Nomad

Breaking the stereotype that digital nomadism is restricted to tech professionals, meet Adrian, a history teacher. He leveraged the virtual teaching boom, packing his comprehensive lessons into an online course. It quickly gained popularity among homeschoolers and education enthusiasts due to its interactive format and unique storytelling approach. His once office-bound job now allows him to visit the historical sites he teaches about, enriching his content with authentic experiences. Adrian admits to initially struggling with the technicality of creating an online course and managing it, but he emphasized the merits of stepping out of your comfort zone.

15.4. Rocking the Start-Up Scene: Victoria and Her Virtual Venture

Victoria, a serial entrepreneur from San Francisco, dived into the digital nomad life not alone, but with her entire team. Under her leadership, her marketing startup embraced a fully remote work model. The liberating work environment saw a surge in productivity and creativity among employees. Victoria ensured regular virtual meet-ups to keep the team connected and even organized annual team retreats to brainstorm and bond in exotic locations. The move proved quite challenging initially, including dealing with stakeholders questioning the unconventional set-up, yet they managed to build a successful company that lives and breathes the digital nomad lifestyle.

15.5. The Fit Nomad: Kenny's Fitness Frenzy

Finally, experience the high-intensity tale of Kenny. A personal trainer hailing from Sydney, he leveraged the paradigm shift to virtual fitness during the pandemic. His YouTube channel featuring innovative home workouts found fans worldwide. Now, he pairs fitness with travel, hosting boot camps in different cities worldwide. Weathering the time-zone troubles, currency challenges, and adapting to local fitness habits have all been part of his spirited journey.

These captivating narratives highlight the diversity underpinning the digital nomad lifestyle – it isn't restricted to specific professions or predispositions. The shared thread among these stories is the audacity to challenge the status quo and adapt to the requirements of this unique lifestyle - liberating them to live a life once believed to be confined to dreams. Though challenges inevitably occur, these nomads exhibit how unshakeable resilience, ceaseless innovation, and a touch of audacity can transform an ordinary desk-bound job into an extraordinary journey spanning the globe.